... where always it's spring...

— SAMUEL COLERIDGE 1776–1834

If I Were a Tree – Signs of Learning®

— *For Stephen* —

Registered Title: Murray David Harwich III

Text ©2012 Mary Belle Harwich

Illustrations ©2012 Sara Groom

ASL Illustrations ©2018 Rosalee Anderson

ALL RIGHTS RESERVED

Printed in the United States

Printed in the United States

Published Frankfort, KY

Book Designs by Marjorie Snelson Design

ISBN 978-0-9830084-9-1

Library of Congress Control Number: 2019913717

To order printed books: www.amazon.com

If I Were a Tree

Signs of Learning®

Story by Mary Belle Harwich

Pictures by Sara Groom

ASL Illustrations by Rosalee Anderson

As straight and tall as a tree can be,
If I were a tree,
What tree would I be?

An oak, the sturdiest of trees?
A willow waving in the breeze?

An apple tree with juicy fruit?
The pine tree in a year-round suit?

A small and tender new green shoot!

Scattering petals for you and me,
If I were a flower,
What kind would I be?

The meadow blossom on the hill?
An orchid? A poppy? A daffodil?

A pure red rose scented sweet?
The bluebell growing trim and neat?

A spray of star-shaped bittersweet!

Slowly crawling for all to see,
If I were a bug,
What bug would I be?

A firefly with its magic light?
A ladybug with wings closed tight?

The cricket leaping rooftop high?
A daddy longlegs ambling by?

Even the dancing butterfly!

Four steady legs
but never three,
If I were an animal,
What kind would I be?

A kangaroo jumping high with glee?
A racing horse beside the sea?

The tawny lion with its rumbling roar?
An elephant building a palace door?

Perhaps the mighty dinosaur!

Raining down so clear and free,
If I were water,
What kind would I be?

The blue-green ocean hatching fish?
A puddle acting as a dish?

A springing brook with its splashing song?
A fast deep river running strong?

Or shall I be the waterfall? —

Cascading down a mossy wall!

Blowing boats across the sea,
If I were a wind,
What wind would I be?

North wind so cold to bring the snow?
South wind that's warm and soft and slow?

A wind for tossing kites up high?
Or sailing leaves into the sky?

And one more wind… do I dare?

A thunder wind to wash the air!

Above the hill, above the tree,
If I were light,
What light would I be?

An orange sun blazing hot and high?
The rainbow reaching across the sky?

A shining star, the moon so round?
A candle glowing near the ground?

A twinkle, a spark, a flash of light?
Some for the day! —

Some for the night!

Skipping, dancing, running free,
If I were a child,
What child would I be?

Helpful or friendly?
Busy or proud?
Laughing or frowning?
Quiet or loud?

Alone or together?

Quite short or quite tall?

Well, maybe, just maybe,

I might be them all!

Signs of Learning

American Sign Lanuage

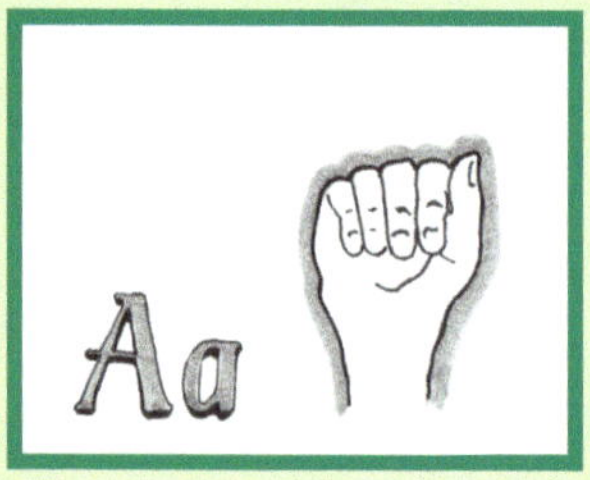
Aa

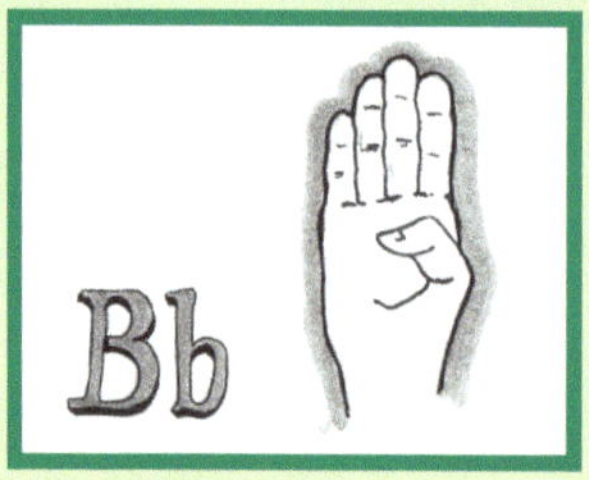
Bb

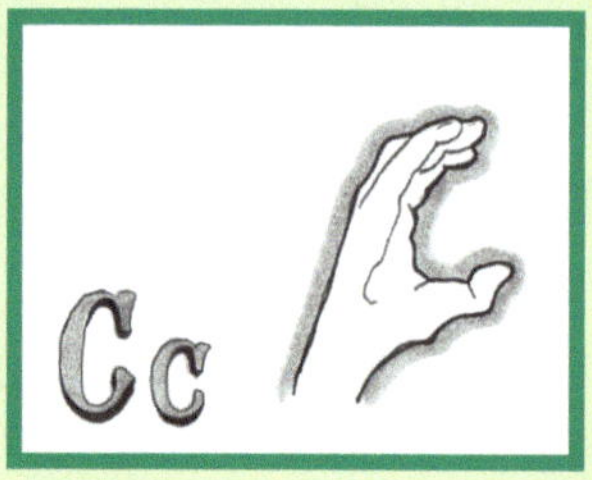
Cc

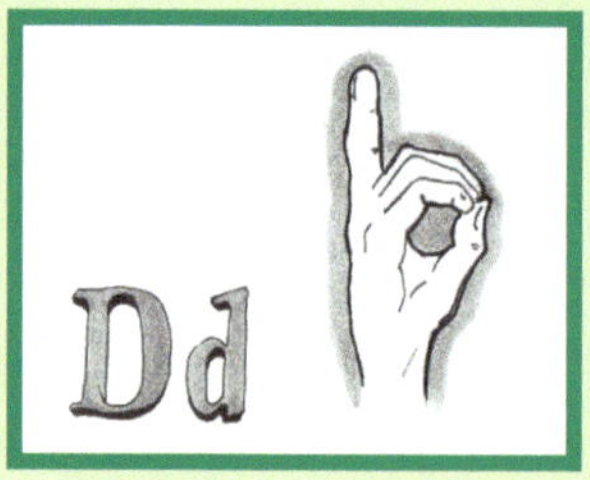
Dd

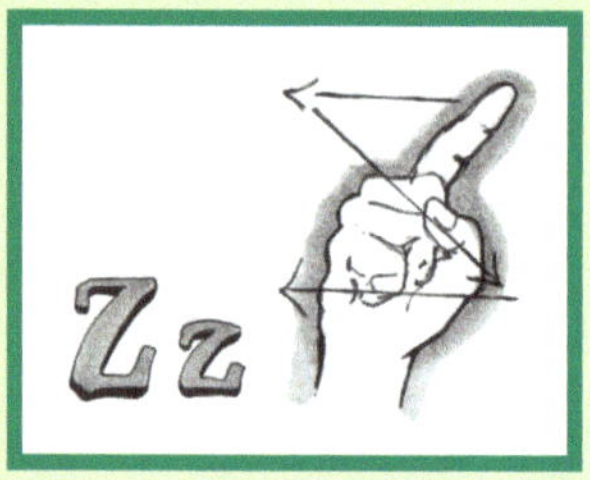
Zz

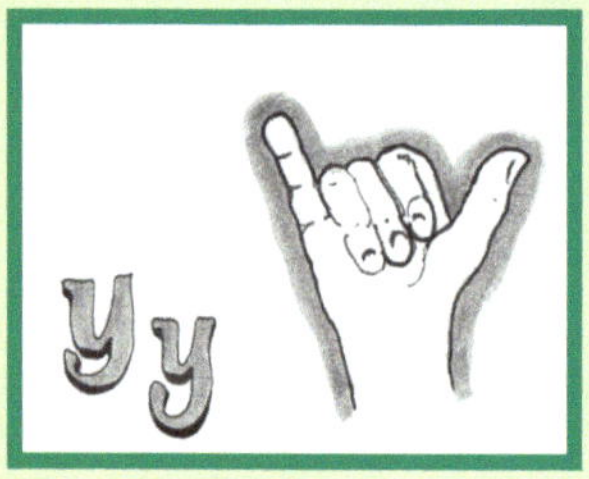
Yy

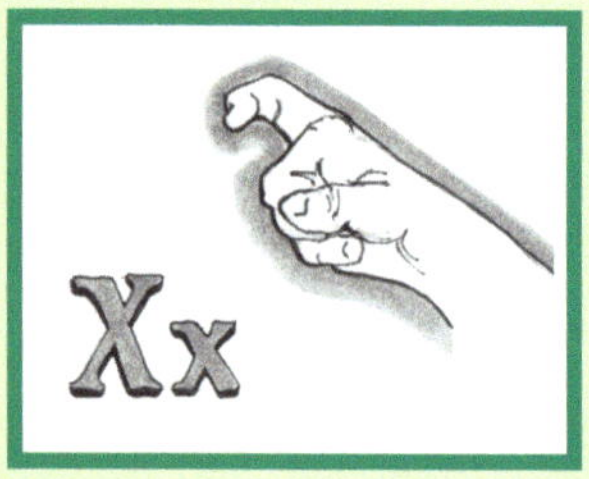
Xx

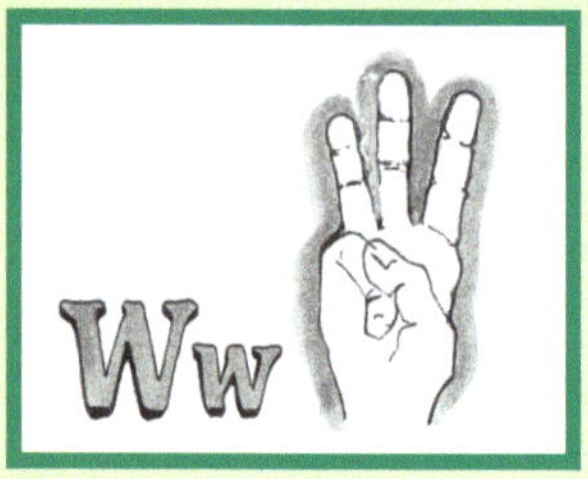
Ww

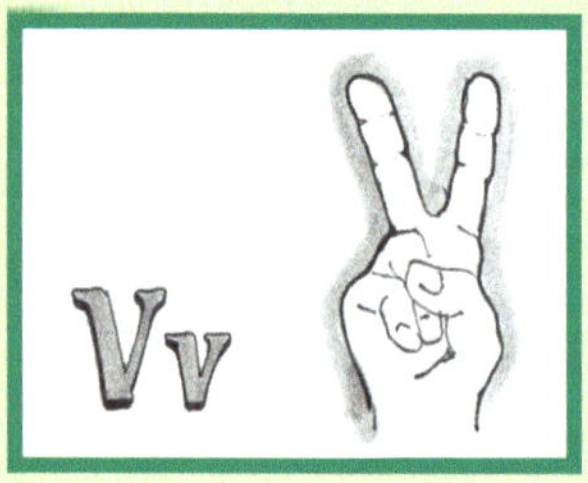
Vv

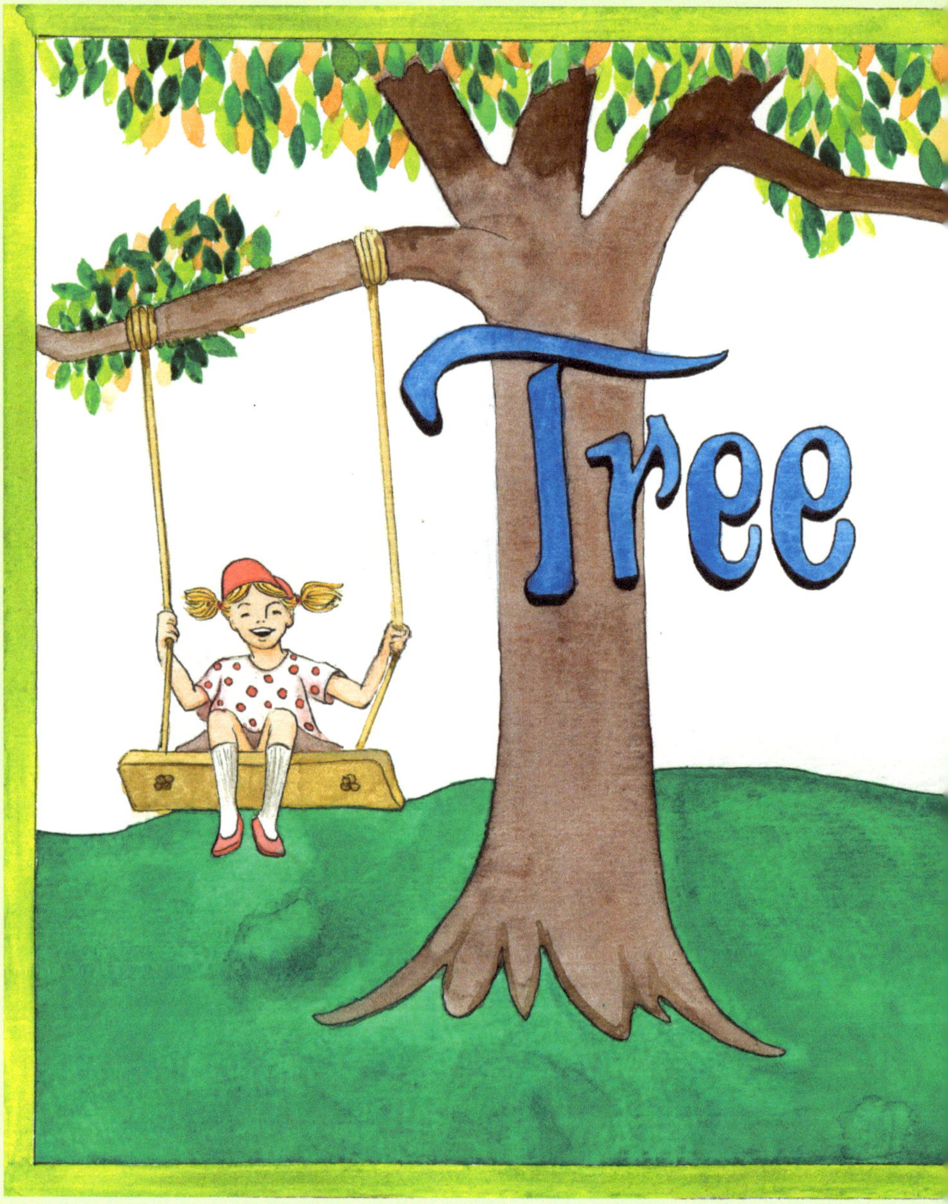
Tree

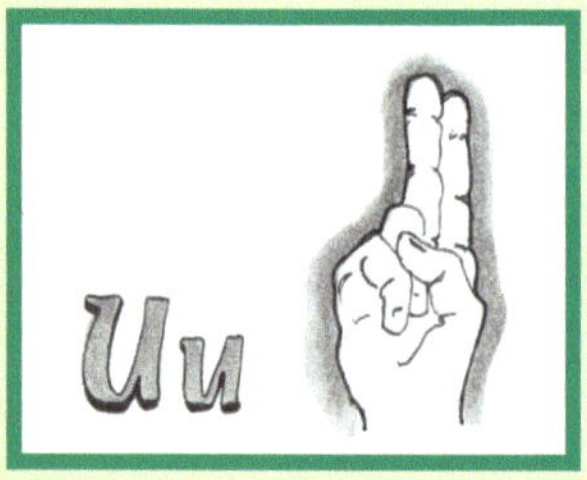
Uu

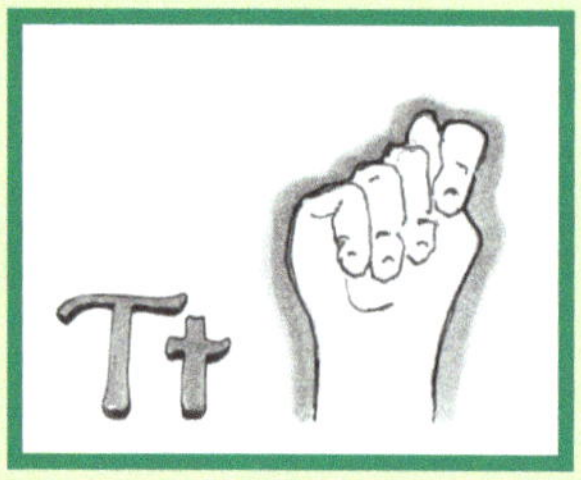
Tt

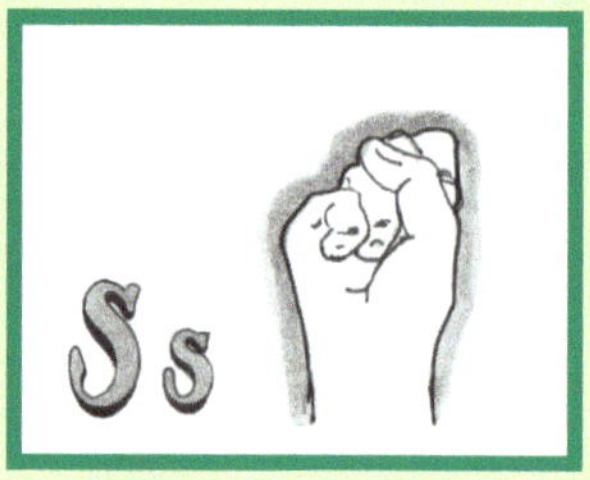
Ss

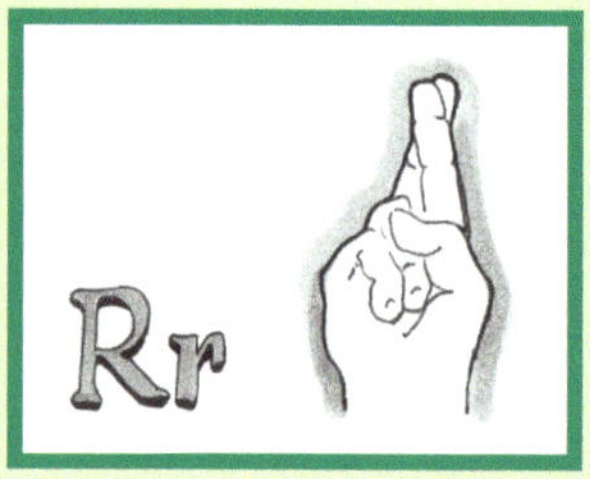
Rr

Ee
Ff
Gg
Hh
Ii
Jj
Kk
Ll
Mm
Nn
Oo
Pp
Qq

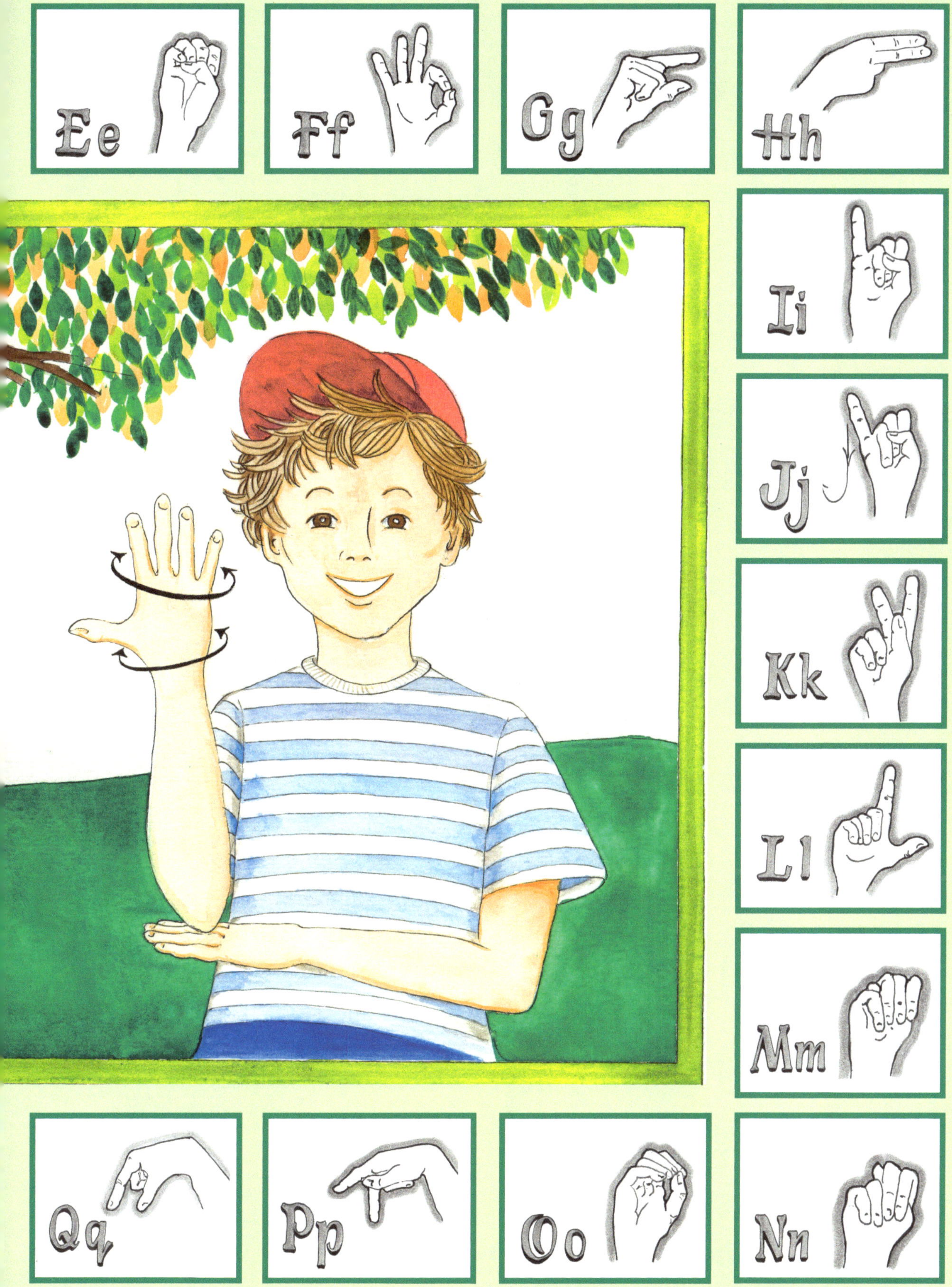

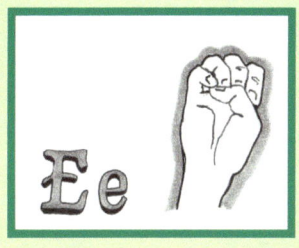

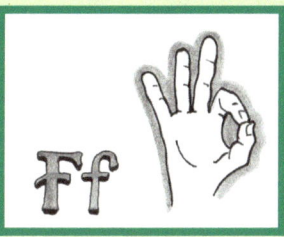

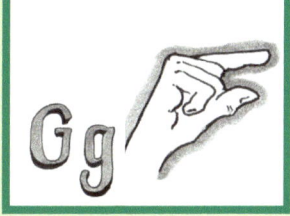

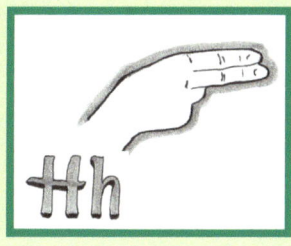

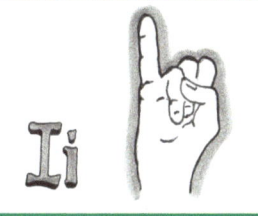

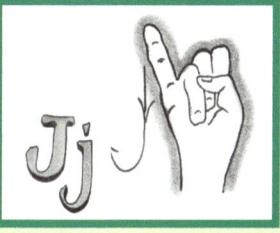

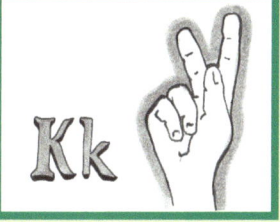

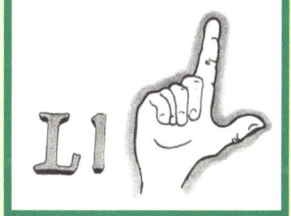

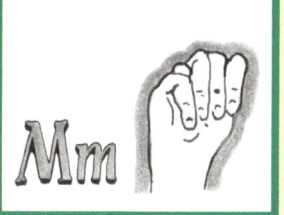

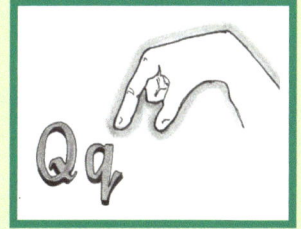

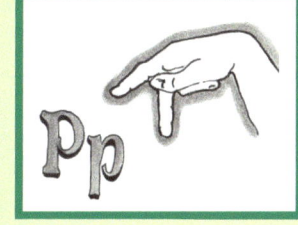

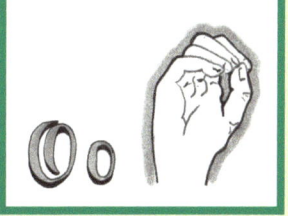

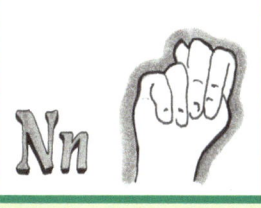

Butterfly

Beetle

Bittersweet

Honey Bee

1 one 2 two 3 three

Counting and adding and subtracting are fun!

Shall we start with a four....4?
Shall we start with a one....1?

Or maybe a two....2?
Or could it be three....3?

You will know in a second what you want it to be!

seven 7   eight 8   nine 9

eleven 11

twelve 12

10
ten

Can you be five?
....5?

Can you be two?
....2?

Look at the clock...

9
nine

eight 8

seven 7

TREE

Well Done!

www.ingramcontent.com/pod-product-compliance
Lightning Source LLC
Chambersburg PA
CBHW041533040426
42446CB00002B/69